THE WHOLE OF POETRY IS PREPOSITION

Claude Royet-Journoud

THE WHOLE OF POETRY
IS PREPOSITION

translated by
Keith Waldrop

LA PRESSE 2011
IOWA CITY & PARIS

La poésie entière est préposition by Claude Royet-Journoud
Copyright © 2007 Éric Pesty Éditeur
Translation copyright © 2011 by Keith Waldrop
All rights reserved

Published in the United States by La Presse,
an imprint of Fence Books

La Presse/Fence Books are distributed by Consortium
www.cbsd.com
www.lapressepoetry.com

Library of Congress Cataloguing in Publication Data
Royet-Journoud, Claude, 1941—
Translated from the French by Keith Waldrop
The Whole of Poetry is Preposition/Claude Royet-Journoud
p.   cm.

ISBN 978-1-934200-45-2
1. French poetry. 2. Poetry. 3. Contemporary translation.

Library of Congress Control Number: 2010941104

First Edition
10 9 8 7 6 5 4 3 2 1

We would like to give warm thanks to Éric Pesty, who first
published this work in book form, for his generosity
in letting us publish this translation.
www.ericpestyediteur.com

These notes were first published by Jean Daive
in his review *Fin* (Pierre Brullé, Paris).

CONTENTS

A CRAFT OF IGNORANCE
(Notes and fragments from interviews)

A writer's immobility puts the world in motion.

To the extent that we hold our gaze still, things move. Thought, as well, exists only with regard to a halt which is empty. Joë Bousquet wrote, *this paralysis has carved a hole in space.* To write is to carve that hole in space. Everything takes off from immobility, from the effort of attention that is also a corporeal effort. The tightrope walker has the same problem; he tries to bring together movement and rest, to find perfect equilibrium. The writer's desk is in the mind, a matter of knowing when to stop, of starting out aware that there is no beginning. Writing is a *craft of ignorance.*

silence is a form

For thought to become act, it must stand still.

"Empty" more of time than of space.

Where does the poem begin? What is there *before* the first line?

The word as "entrance" and "scene."

Poetry: what proceeds without incident.

Note well the absence of "denouement."

I don't write until I find the preceding book illegible.

All writing is built on entropy. The only question is the one of sense, and that is insoluble. Sense has to be caught the moment it develops, while it remains still undetermined.

Charles Bernstein seems to insist on the sonority of verse, of words. As for me, I would insist on the absence of assonance, alliteration, image, etc. I would look for a certain "flatness." But our two approaches perhaps converge in our precise and ambiguous concern for *sense*. Could this be the same concern seen from opposite perspectives?

Replacing the image with the *word* image.

The cocked ear always hears mother!

What word to replace "meditation"?

Poem $\left\{ \begin{array}{l} \text{sound (waking)} \\ \text{sight} \\ \text{memory (energy)} \end{array} \right.$

This shifty death.

First I write prose of no literary interest. The poem does not come from the prose, but it will not come without the prose, which is merely "cleaning," making it possible to see.

Prose is childhood. It's a wake-up call. Escape from blindness. But all that explains nothing. There is no visible connection between the initial prose and the published poem. No manuscript shows any real state of the text in process of becoming.

There is also a job of suppression. Which is not to claim that under the text there is some other text hiding out. The suppression merely permits theatricalizing certain words, certain projects, allowing them more easily a concrete form.

I write down something barely visible: there lies the menace, where something violent may be born. Bataille says the philosopher is someone who is afraid. Some books are overdressed. To write is to unveil the anatomy. The literal has to be followed through.

I like Aristotle and Wittgenstein. I used to think it was because I had not understood them. Now I think it's because they are simple, detailed, finicky. Trifles fascinate me. Pushing the literal to its extreme, as Wittgenstein does, we trip into terror.

The trick is to be literal (not metaphorical). To weigh the language in its "minimal" units of meaning. For me, Eluard's line, *The earth is blue like an orange*, tires, dragged down by an overload of meaning. Whereas, for example, *The wall behind is a wall of chalk*, by Marcelin Pleynet stands, and continues to stand, I think, by its very exactitude and, taken of course in context, paradoxically, unfixed in meaning, thus holding for anyone an abiding fiction.

To bring out the part of the body that writes (to make it visible, legible): arm, wrist, hand, finger, mouth... To inscribe it in the fable, make of it a character in the plot. As if that were the whole matter: the hand becoming separate from the body by writing. And the cold.

I have the impression that this book (*Les objets contiennent l'infini*) is a hesitation between inner and outer, pre-natal; the moment when the body is neither in nor out. The "balance" between verse and prose is an image of that. (Verse or prose could perhaps return, by the poem, to the act of birth, if that could be done.)

Placement, as Saint Augustine might say, is impossible. That is why, on the page, it must be precise, exact.

Fear brings us together. Fear of discussing the book that I write and you read. Or again, the opposite. A "true" word has been claimed. But when will it come around again?

Our body looks flat to us, two-dimensional. Then the instant the heart, emotions, enter into play we gain density. Density sometimes means writing a book, but may also be the point at which you're not sure you can do it.

Italics, quotation marks — they provide a minimal theatricalization. The italic, for me, has a phallic quality; its tilt a form of exhibition. Something to rip the page, put there to be conspicuous, to underline.

The science of fossil tracks (ichnology), in which the shape and weight of a prehistorical animal are figured, is not so far from my way of working.

I connect one gesture to another.

The book "turns" on certain unsettled terms — where the word is searching for definition by the reader.

A real landscape — stretch of sight (i.e., knowledge, prehension). Another, in the mind. From appeasement, in some sense, to the menace.

The *menace* without which there would be no thought.

Plot is the tissue that separates and realigns four or five character-words.

It's always being asked why a poem ends. It exists when recognized, as we "recognize" a body in the morgue. Something frightening and strange. It's when that snaps off. You recognize something absent, withdrawn just at the moment the poem is anonymous enough for you to sign it.

[FOR EMILIO ARAÚXO]

"the body bears the vacancy of the fiction that distinguishes it"

Anne-Marie Albiach.

To come back to a book as back into a room after long absence. Placing the breath for the body's displacement.

Emotion coursing the body, as in sudden bounds of memory. What does space retain of all that?

A few gestures that sum up nothing.

The "preparation" that makes it possible to end blindness (maybe).

Words come only to the dismantled (Collobert, for example). What we're in for is a dismantling gone mad. Mad because of its extreme mobility — precipitation characterizes it — and because we love it without *reason*.

Is it perhaps only forms that come to us.

"There is nothing astonishing in my not being able to explain the poem except by itself; in other words, that *I cannot explain it*." (Pseudo-Wittgenstein)

Must the language always be the other's?

Comings and goings of the mental and of the fable.

In order for this to hold together the space of a few seconds, the space of a body or a movement within the body.

To found a *real* on the metaphorical! I prefer surface, the flat and, frankly, the platitude, since it alone forces the world to answer.

What is written is mute.

You must learn to follow your own hand.

The word END, so that what follows becomes what precedes.

— Why have you chosen silence?
— (After having refused to reply to several questions, Ezra Pound's lips move slightly, half open; gently, sadly, he says:) It's the silence which has chosen me.

For a long time, I didn't know my name. Despite my ignorance, the name was mine.
(Is it like that for a book title?)

Money and darkness as stroke of unity, of language.

Writing: to join spans of time.

Displacing the world, not by changing the word, but by repeating it.

Starting from the notion of *indivisibility*, to develop an idea of the line, of the sequence, of the book.

I borrow as much from Revelation as from Bescherelle, from Simenon as much as from the *Roman de la Rose*, from Lola as from Saint Augustine or Hallâj, from an old lady jabbering in a café in Clichy as from Merleau-Ponty, from a guy walking along muttering to himself as from Georges Gougenheim or Wittgenstein.

No metaphor, rather an indicator. Is it from the absence of metaphor that narration is born. (The plot.)

We only "verify" commonplaces.

Form as excess of emotion.

Jack Spicer: *Metaphors are not for humans.*

Jean Daive, on my answering machine: *Words no longer recognize me.*

TO DISCRIMINATE

The whole of poetry is preposition.

It's only with your foot on the core of the tightrope that the narrative unfolds. Before that, there are only fragments of sense and you see nothing of what ties the plot together.

Voice is no help in constructing a framework. It dissolves the whole, makes it fragile, and retains only appearance.

Accidents are essential. They are what give form and readability.

"They speak to the ear, I wish to speak to the memory." (Joseph Joubert.)

Too much sense reduces the line to ashes.

In the hollows of language. Never in its fullness.

("Je" is all the more present in *Les natures indivisibles* as in *La notion d'obstacle* this pronoun is totally absent.)

Importance of the back.

A book is not a property. Whose property is a body?

"My science can only be a science point by point. I have neither time nor means to trace a continuous line." (Marcel Jousse.)

The body is not a subject; that's why...

OF THE PREPOSITION

Sense in suspense. In abeyance. Sense is constructed from a distance.

There is a sensation I find hard to grasp, to comprehend. But sometimes I feel it touch me.

To define how this arrives? A confused mass. We turn this way and that. We try to build something from scraps. Something unpredictable is hatching in order to prolong the plot.

I would really like to come clear as to what happens "before" and "after" the preposition. Why in the very articulation sense becomes magnetic. The elbow makes the arm, the knee the leg! Everything surges towards articulation.

Essential because transparent.

The importance of the preposition, for me, comes perhaps also from the fact that I clip all other articulations. I want to superpose senses, bring up intersections.

All this tends to be extremely awkward. I mean in the elaboration of a form. What is awkward is the heart.

The preposition is a little like rhyme! It puts the sense into play.

The preposition in any translation... (For example, that of the Bible.)

Prepositions of Louis Zukofsky.

"Act of moving forward."

PASTE-ON

A blind part necessary, fruitful.

"It's inserting the poetic that brings to light the brute separation of language and being. Language, even *worn down*, presents only itself: a wall." (Daniel Oster.)

Begun by the hands...

A word *in private* sent only eye to eye. (A sort of curtain lowering.) It need not be read. It's understood mentally. That's it.

I like this resistance (to sense).

"Just like plunging a finger into the soil to recognize what land we're in, I poke my finger into life: it has the odor of nothing." (Kierkegaard.)

"All time together forms a single day in God's economy."
(Hamann.)

Unheard verticality in Roger Lewinter's sentences.

Sleep. Dividing.

"Things have a place, but perception is nowhere..."
(Merleau-Ponty.)

The placement of hinges. The preposition allows for
expansion.

"Heart" will appear 3 times in the first 3 sequences,
then not at all in the 3 following, to come 3 times
again in the very last.

in the dark you count

"Because they know all the words, they think they know all the verities." (Joseph Joubert.)

I too, often, remain *outside*.

Books don't exist.

The text has a skin, an epidermis. The slightest typographical variation (roman, italic, hyphen, etc.) plays no inconsiderable role.

The book needs no voice.
Reading aloud is a little like looking at an autograph text. It lacks the *neutrality* of print, which is what makes the sense burst forth.

"...the page must first be seen in order to be made invisible." (Michael Davidson.)

"In fact, to say that beginning is the act by which we begin, is giving a pretty lame explanation." (Kierkegaard.)

"There are as many things in a sentence as there are behind it." (Wittgenstein.)

The sentence has to come back to what the head anticipates, what the rhythm demands.

Between air and water, there must be the preposition.

To seize time again by the tail.

Recurring imprints ...

The wish to see the design of the poem rather than the poem. To feel its weight on the paper.

I have no language for anything else (than what I do).

Sense rushes into the preposition.

The only "truth," movement. Movement, not rhythm.

To subject certain words to an equilibrium always being reinvented.

To describe what allowed "bipedal locomotion," Claudine Cohen speaks of a "succession of avoided falls."

Searching out accidents which language continually provokes under the surface.

Sentences, fragments of sentences, wait for years for their proper place.

Absence of conjugation. (Stacking phrases. Super-imposing them to gear down the narrative.)

Why work so hard to find the *weakest* link.

How worm out the plot which vibrates inside the text. Which stammers. Which is trying to find a form, a way to breathe.

Some words suddenly stand out. They signal their exhaustion, their too extended use.

"The real and the true are two different things." (Robert Bresson.)

"But this importance cannot be in what the poem says, since in that case the fact that it is a poem would be a redundancy. The importance lies in what the poem *is*." (William Carlos Williams.)

"So to mistake the rhythm of a sentence is to mistake the very sense of the sentence." (Nietzsche.)

"We read because within us there are unmouthed words." (Michèle Cohen-Halimi.)

The narrative is in the preposition.

Things under-the-tongue, like things under-the-table!

"Now it is not the case that everything we say is said with the point entirely clear; more often our mouth speaks by itself." (Wittgenstein.)

This is the seventh title in the La Presse series
of contemporary French poetry in translation.
The series is edited by Cole Swensen.
The book is set in Adobe Jenson and
was designed by Shari DeGraw.